Birmingham's monument to Admiral Lord Nelson (Sir R. Westmacott, 1809) is the earliest surviving civic tribute to the victor of the Battle of Trafalgar in 1805. Local Quaker influence and finance for the memorial ensured that its tone would not be triumphalist. The near-perfect modelling of the figure does not sacrifice accuracy for style.

War Memorials in Britain

Jim Corke

To Una Marie Corke, a daughter of the Dockyard.

Published by Shire Publications Ltd,
Midland House, West Way, Botley, Oxford OX2 0PH, UK.
(Website: www.shirebooks.co.uk)

Copyright © 2005 by Jim Corke.
First published 2005. Transferred to digital print on
demand 2011.
Shire Library 441. ISBN 978 0 74780 626 4.
Jim Corke is hereby identified as the author of this work in
accordance with Section 77 of the Copyright, Designs and
Patents Act 1988.

British Library Cataloguing in Publication Data:
Corke, Jim
War memorials in Britain. – (Shire library; 441)
1. War memorials – Great Britain – History
I. Title 355.1'6'0941
ISBN-10: 0 7478 0626 8
ISBN-13: 978 0 74780 626 4

Cover: Large Victory war memorial in Rougement gardens, Exeter (near Queen St, Central Station). Photograph courtesy of Andrew Head.

ACKNOWLEDGEMENTS
All photographs are from the author's collection save for the one of Sueno's Stone (Valentine & Sons, Dundee). The author wishes to thank all those who provided information on and access to individual memorials, including: the Trustees of the Battle of Britain Memorial; the National Memorial Arboretum; Trinity Arts Centre; the borough councils and museum departments of Ashford (Kent), Charnwood, Medway, Portsmouth, Stockport and Swale; the Commonwealth War Graves Commission; churchwardens and officers of churches great and small; English Heritage; the Faversham Society; the War Memorials Trust (formerly known as Friends of War Memorials); the Imperial War Museum (UK National Inventory of War Memorials); the Ministry of Defence (Army); the Port of London Police; the regimental secretaries and curators of military museums; and the staff of the Scottish National War Memorial.

Printed in Great Britain by PrintOnDemand-Worldwide.com, Peterborough, UK.

Contents

The road to remembrance 4

Long stones and high crosses 20

Liminal lights 28

Singularities 36

Monumentalists 42

Further reading 49

Gazetteer 50

Index 64

A young 'Jock' sits facing the Scottish National War Memorial high above him in Edinburgh Castle, appearing to tell his story while others unfold around him (Tait Mackenzie, 1927). On the frieze behind him, Scots Americans are shown responding to the call from their kinsfolk during the First World War.

The road to remembrance

It seems probable that one of the purposive reasons for the erection of ancient megaliths in Britain was the veneration of ancestors killed in battle. It is certain that among the public monumentalia constructed during the Roman occupation of Britain were sophisticated monuments to Victory, and that Roman cemeteries were replete with military mementos mori. While the later Saxon kingdoms are notable for their lack of memorial artefacts, the Celtic regions outside their control continued with the ancient tradition of raising 'long stones'. The carvings on Pictish examples often display scenes of battle as well as Christian symbols. Echoes of these early examples of commemoration are detectable in the war memorials of the twentieth century, notably those created in the wake of the First World War, the most productive period for remembrance. The extensive church-building programme of the Normans and their successors provided an opportunity for the new military elites to construct monuments for their dead in a manner which persisted for centuries, at the same time imprinting their dominant presence on local communities. The practice was interrupted by the Reformation and again ceased during the interregnum which followed the execution of Charles I. At the Restoration in 1660 his equestrian statue was installed on the site where those who had voted for his death were themselves executed. This marked the start of an enduring tradition of public monumentalia, in which, as a means to an end, the images of kings and their military commanders were elevated on horseback, pillars and plinths, and monuments were restored to churches. It effectively both promoted the authority of the State and raised the profile of its rulers by displaying them as secular icons in an expansionist Britain.

In order to secure possession of his regained kingdom, Charles II founded a standing army, the first since the departure of the Roman legions, and reformed the navy. Both were used to spearhead the drive for Empire, in which trade followed the flag and Thomas Atkins and Jack Tar would leave their bones to whiten on many a foreign field or

During the regeneration of central London, 1829–41, it was decided to dedicate its largest square to Nelson's great victory at Trafalgar. His monument, probably the best-known landmark in Britain, took another thirty years or so to complete. His statue (Baily) tops a 150 foot fluted Corinthian column (Railton), towering over the equestrian figure of Charles I (Le Sueur), which preceded it on this site by two hundred years.

among the corals. As part of the plan to build a capital city fit for the new Britain, Christopher Wren designed the Royal Hospitals at Chelsea and Greenwich, not mere hospices for a few indigent in-pensioners but part of a grander scheme. In effect they became the first national war memorials. The final defeat of Napoleon in 1815 opened the door to a golden age of imperial expansion and unprecedented prosperity for Britain, when memorials to those other than the great and famous were gradually introduced.

Not a year of the long reign of Queen Victoria passed when her forces were not engaged somewhere in the world gaining or retaining territory and trade. The logistical impossibility of repatriating Britons from faraway places with strange-sounding names led to an expansion in memorialisation as a substitute for burial in Britain. This development was facilitated by the growth of religious revivalism accompanied by urban growth, when many overcrowded, insanitary churchyards were closed to burials and new cemeteries were built. In the 1820s many old, dilapidated churches were 'restored' in *faux* Gothic style while many new ones were built by public subscription and under the government's programme of building 'Waterloo' churches as a counter to disorder and dissent in the expanding towns. Comrades and kin of an increasing number of Britons who had served

The gilded figure of Charles II in Roman dress (Grinling Gibbons, 1676) faces the Royal Hospital, Chelsea, which he founded and his niece, Mary II, completed. Beneath Wren's classical portico and colonnade are war memorials, including those to men of the Corps of Pensioners, 1689–1803, killed on active service, and victims of air raids on the premises in both world wars.

Above: *Edinburgh's 'Parthenon' on Calton Hill overlooks the 'Athens of the North'. Intended to replicate Pericles' Temple to Athena, it is not the ruin it appears but a project to commemorate Scots of all ranks who fell in the Peninsular War of 1807–14, but which was left unfinished in the 1820s when public subscriptions dried up.*

Great Yarmouth's 144 foot fluted Doric column was dedicated to 'Norfolk's Own', chiefly Nelson, its most famous son, who was born at Burnham Thorpe. Britannia and her handmaidens top the column (Wilkins, 1919), she with her back to the sea and facing his birthplace, where, according to rumour, he had wished to be buried. The original Coade stone figures have been replaced in glass fibre.

That most ancient of war memorial forms, a burial mound, is recalled in the grounds of the St George's Centre, Gillingham, Kent, formerly a naval church. In 1904 the bodies of 521 Napoleonic prisoners of war, buried in a nearby cemetery, were brought here, together with their monument; another 323 were added in 1991 when St Mary's Island was sold for housing development.

overseas took the opportunity to erect memorials for those they could not repatriate, helping to revive medieval church decoration.

The Victorian middle classes saw it as their moral and social duty to erect enduring mementos mori in the new necropolises. Enterprising firms of monumental masons published copious catalogues, inviting bespoke orders and keeping stock items available for personalisation. From producing hosts of angels, thickets of crosses and avenues of obelisks and other funerary forms it took only a small leap of faith for them to develop a niche market in war memorials.

Once a 'Waterloo' church (Decimus Burton, 1829), Tunbridge Wells' Trinity Arts Centre has a fine wall monument to Lieutenant Newton, who died of wounds at Maharajpur in 1845 (R. Westmacott junior). Another, by the same hand, at All Saints Church in Maidstone commemorates officers and men who fell at Ramnagar three years later.

An elaborate monument to the three Guards regiments (Bell, 1859), who lost some twenty thousand men in the Crimea, mainly from disease. The figures were cast from the metal of guns captured at Sevastopol, some of which are piled at the rear of this monument in Lower Regent Street in London, an uncommon practice for memorials in Britain.

The growing prosperity of Victorian towns caused many local dignitaries to push for city status, while many self-made industrialists sought immortality in architecture. Municipal buildings were constructed on a grand scale in a pastiche of the Classical and Gothic revivals. Environmentally friendly public parks and gardens sprouted bandstands and belvederes, while 'statumania' imported from Europe informed sculptural works. Everywhere, the Victorian potential for promoting local and national achievements and restoring loss of face evidenced the new, confident zeitgeist.

Military and political incompetence in the Crimea and elsewhere, allied to the fear of

At 31 feet, the Maiwand Lion in Reading (Simonds, 1886) was believed at the time it was installed to be the largest in the world. It tops a sarcophagal base on which are recorded the names of 328 officers and men of the Berkshire Regiment killed in the retreat from Kabul. The lone survivor, a mongrel dog named Bobby, was decorated at Windsor by Queen Victoria.

Left: *The monument to the King's Own Scottish Borderers (Birnie Rhind, 1906) on Edinburgh's North Bridge pays tribute to those who fell in campaigns from India to South Africa between 1878 and 1902. The officer and men in this 'last stand' pose are wearing regulation pattern uniforms of the Boer War developed from Indian Army equipment.*

Right: *A standard Victorian monumental wall brass is enlivened here by cameos in burnished copper (Challcott, 1904) showing men of The Buffs and Imperial Yeomanry in the role of mounted infantry in the Boer War. It was commissioned by the burgesses of Margate and hung in the town hall, now a museum of local history.*

invasion from a resurgent France, produced a traditional British military response. The near-moribund Militia was revived, and Volunteer and Yeomanry regiments that had been disbanded after 1813 were remustered. The public drills and 'war-games' of these enthusiastic amateurs provided much popular free entertainment while at the same time raising the profile of the military. In 1899 'Tommy' embarked for the Cape on a high tide of jingoism with a press corps for escort. It was, however, the Boers who hit the headlines as they thinned the British lines, in khaki now not red, necessitating a call for reinforcements. With the regulars in short supply, the amateurs stepped into the breach. When relief came they returned to Britain and a heroes' welcome. Once again, military deficiencies had been exposed but a thousand or so war memorials helped to paper over the cracks.

A rising tide of European militarism led to calls in Britain for universal conscription. Instead, the Militia was converted into a Special Reserve and the Volunteers and Yeomanry into a new Territorial

'The Response' (Goscombe John, 1923) in Newcastle upon Tyne's city centre is amongst the finest monuments of the First World War. Commissioned privately, it shows citizens responding to Kitchener's famous call to arms. On the reverse, in stone, St George is supported on one hand by a Royal Northumberland Fusilier in 1914 pattern uniform and on the other by a soldier in the uniform of 1674, the year the regiment was first raised.

Force, which included women. In 1914 a British Expeditionary Force comprising mainly regulars and reservists went to France to serve under Allied command. It was intended that they would be strengthened incrementally by the 'New Armies' to be formed from those who volunteered in response to Kitchener's famous appeal. By the end of 1915 some two and a half million had come forward but no great number found their way to the Front until the following year.

Throughout 1915 the 'Old Contemptibles', as they were popularly known, fought with distinction until tactics of attrition took their toll. Heavy Allied losses caused the High Command, fearful of the impact on public morale of so many funerals, to ban the repatriation of the dead for the duration of the war. Battlefield burials became the order of the day just as Britons were conscripted for the

The war memorial in Bushey, Hertfordshire, features the figure of a woman in classical mourning pose (Reid Dick, 1922). It stands in a small, neat garden of remembrance by the side of a main road. On the back of this lesser-known work by a leading creator of public statuary between the world wars are inscribed rolls of honour.

On top of a massive pedestal in Devon granite at Exeter's Northernhay Park, Victory, with sword and wreath in hand, tramples a dragon underfoot (Angel, 1923). Her figure and that of a chained prisoner at the foot of the monument won critical acclaim at the Royal Academy's Exhibition in 1922.

first time. Within months men were in action on the Somme and the death toll for the first day of the offensive exceeded that for the entire Boer War, adding to some six thousand lost only weeks earlier in the indecisive naval action off Jutland. A pall of mourning shrouded Britain, itself the subject of naval bombardment and air raids that had caused civilian casualties since the start of the war.

The Imperial War Graves Commission was constituted in 1917 with a remit to design and construct military cemeteries, and later to commission the building of monuments especially for the 'missing', those with no known grave. The government encouraged local communities to form committees to raise funds for their own memorials but offered little advice and imposed few restrictions, while promoting the efficacy of religious images as a way of achieving catharsis. Commercial and industrial sponsors, naval and military associations and private patrons contributed to an eclectic mix of conventional and idiosyncratic memorials. Mourning for the loss of a generation of mainly young men is present in nearly all of them but there is a leavening of those that overtly celebrate victory through the

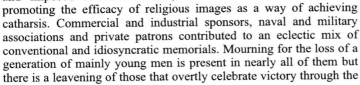

The main entrance of Waterloo station in London commemorates staff of the London & South Western Railway in the form of a triumphal arch (Szlumper, 1922). At the attic level, Britannia presides over allegorical groups representing War and Peace (Whiffen). The clock is both a timepiece and a metaphor for life and death.

As a basis for Keswick's memorial, its locally born creator, Derwent Wood, chose a Roman cemetery stele (1923). Here, Victory wears the Phrygian cap commonly associated with Mithras, god of the Roman legions. On the reverse, a plaque commemorates employees of the now defunct Cockermouth, Keswick & Penrith Railway Company.

use of allegorical female figures and martial saints slaying dragons.

Smaller towns and many villages opted for simpler, less ostentatious tributes, usually in the form of crosses but also solitary military figures resting on rifles reversed, symbolic of 'Everyman' and popularised in the Boer War memorials. No town and only a very few villages lacked a memorial of some kind, though some of the smallest communities pooled their resources for a combined project. The repetition of family names adds particular poignancy to many of these memorials.

The popular figure of a solitary soldier resting on his rifle reversed was the choice of the holiday resort of Thornton Cleveleys in Lancashire. To accommodate those who fell in the Second World War, imaginative use was made of large open books, on which their names are inscribed, set around the original memorial.

The eastern end of Glasgow's commodious George Square is taken up by the elaborate façade of the Municipal Offices, in front of which a large cenotaph is set in a precinct guarded by two lions (Burnet, 1922). During the First World War the site was occupied by a recruiting office, where volunteers and conscripts in their tens of thousands came to enlist.

The signing of the Treaty of Versailles officially ending the war in 1919 was accompanied by a ceremonial parade in London with Whitehall turned into an Avenue of Remembrance by an assortment of temporary tributes. Among them, Lutyens's Cenotaph caught the eye, not least because it acted as the main saluting base for the march past. Its 'empty-tomb' concept, derived from ancient Egypt via Greece, caught the imagination of all those familiar with the ban on repatriation, extended in perpetuity. Sensing this, the government commissioned its reconstruction in Portland stone, and the following year it was dedicated as the official memorial for all the fallen of the British Empire and became the

Bude's memorial tops the natural, if diminutive, Sholden Hills, which have the appearance of ancient burial mounds. Its pylon is topped by a Greco-Roman lamp and its face is decorated with bayonets reversed (Marsden, 1922). Lutyens is said to have considered using such a lamp, but with an ever-burning flame, for his Cenotaph in Whitehall.

This large cemetery cross in Faversham, Kent, marks the mass grave of most of those killed by the worst accident in the four hundred years of the town's explosives industry, which occurred on Easter Sunday 1916. In all, 108 died, all of them men, since by law women were prohibited from working in the factory on Sundays.

Warrior, a white gelding, went to France with the 'Old Contemptibles' in 1914. Despite being wounded by shrapnel, he recovered to serve out the war. In 1919 he was found a home at Southampton police stables, where he died in 1936. Some 350,000 horses and mules died on the Western Front; none apart from Warrior received individual recognition. His memorial stone is at the Southampton Municipal Golf Course.

This Mark IV tank at Ashford, Kent, is a solitary survivor of those presented to towns that were deemed to have made significant contributions to victory in the First World War. It owes its survival in part to having been used for some years as an electricity substation! In 1987 it was renovated and provided with a protective shelter by Army Engineers.

Hailed as a masterwork, the Royal Artillery Monument in London's Hyde Park (Jagger, 1925) features a monstrous howitzer on a massive plinth (Pearson) attended by larger-than-life gunners. One of them is shown dead beneath his greatcoat at ground level, an unusual feature. The sculptor clearly drew on his active service with the Artists' Rifles on the Western Front and at Gallipoli.

focus for subsequent annual Remembrance Day parades. Its deceptively simple design and deliberately non-sectarian message ensured that its form would be adopted more widely, with local variations.

Few among the cheering crowds that greeted the declaration of war in 1914 could have foreseen the cost in terms of lives lost and those permanently disabled. Some had even believed it would be 'over by Christmas'. Six million had gone to war and one in ten was posted dead or missing. Most casualties came not from bayonets or bullets but from the 'monstrous anger of the guns'. Trains and trucks served men and guns, increasingly replacing horses and mules. Tanks first appeared on the Front in 1916 although aircraft had flown from the start.

Total war, including deliberate attacks on civilian targets by Zeppelins and Gotha bombers, was a new experience for Britons in general and women in particular. Women not only staffed hospitals and drove ambulances but were drafted to work in fields and factories and voluntarily filled other jobs left vacant by men. By the end of the war they were being directly recruited into Auxiliary Services supporting the Army, Navy and Air Force. After 1916 unrestricted submarine warfare cost many lives among the Merchant Marine and brought Britons to the brink of starvation. Such experiences caused an irreversible shift in attitudes to memorialisation.

The National Monument to Britain's Merchant Marine and Fishing Fleets (Lutyens, 1928) was built on Tower Hill, not alongside the Thames as envisaged. When the Commonwealth War Graves Commission added a sunken precinct (Maufe, 1955) with statues (Whiffen) after the Second World War, to commemorate a threefold increase in casualties, the appearance of the site was enhanced.

The nation as a whole expected that memorials would recognise the contribution of the many and that they would occupy the highroads in towns and villages. The equestrian statue of Earl Haig was an anachronism years before it was erected in Whitehall in 1937. Local memorial committees chose prominent sites for their commemoration of local people, some choosing to effect remembrance by providing services for the living, notably hospitals and public amenities, despite some stiff opposition from traditionalists.

Above: *Oldham's impressive First World War monument (Toft, 1921) stands on a high bank in a precinct formed by the churchyard wall of the parish church, on which are recorded the names of the fallen. Following the Second World War the base was modified to accommodate a book of remembrance viewed via a window, its pages being turned mechanically.*

Right: *The bare-headed, long-striding soldier represents 'Coming Home' (Tait Mackenzie, 1922). Prominently sited at a crossroads in Cambridge, the memorial is dedicated to the 'Men of Cambridgeshire, the Isle of Ely, the Borough and University of Cambridge'.*

The Freemasons' Hall in London was dedicated as a memorial to all Freemasons killed in the First World War. Opened in 1933, it houses a museum, library, offices and meeting rooms. On the first floor is a richly decorated hall of memory with rolls of honour and a colourful stained glass window. It is probably the grandest and most costly memorial in Britain.

The unfinished business of the First World War was resumed in 1939 on a truly global scale. This time, despite greater industrialisation of war and new weapons of mass destruction, the military suffered fewer casualties while civilian loss of life escalated; by mid 1941 forty-three thousand had died in the Blitz alone. When the Second World War ended in 1945 there was no new rush to remembrance: people expected what scarce resources there were to be used for the rebuilding of homes and the provision of work. Many felt that a bomb-scarred landscape and the addition of new names to old memorials would suffice, at least in the short term. Special cases such as a new generation of 'missing', primarily aircrew and those lost at sea, merited substantial extensions to existing memorials and some major new works. Special-interest groups who felt their cause to have been largely neglected, such as the Burma Star and Far East Prisoners of War Associations, took matters into their own hands.

The Korean War of 1950–3 was the last of the old-style conflicts and the last in which National Servicemen fought a conventional war. During the Cold War Britons served mainly under United Nations or NATO command, but they were also called upon to

Close to St Paul's Cathedral a memorial was belatedly erected to firefighters who died in the Second World War, many in the Blitz (Mills, 1991). Their names are recorded on the base, which also carries a relief recording twenty-three women who died in service. In 2003 it was rededicated as the Firefighters' National Memorial.

The Air Forces Memorial at historic Runny-mede, Surrey (Maufe, 1953), commemorates some twenty thousand 'missing' who operated from bases in Britain and north-west Europe in the Second World War. Their names are recorded on the walls of circular cloisters leading from a triple-arched entrance to a vaulted shrine under the tower. On its inward face are the figures of Justice, Victory and Courage (Hill), which look down on a war-stone.

cover Britain's withdrawal from its imperial role, reversing the position of a century earlier. From 1960 there was a return to all-regular forces and it was they who garrisoned Belize against invasion and recovered the Falklands in 1982. The memorials of these years reflect changed times and altered cases and the remedying of some lacunas in remembrance.

Memorials generally, and monuments in particular, reflect the image that those who created them wished to project in their own time and for posterity, providing evidence of how they expected

This memorial in Woodhall Spa in Lincolnshire (Stevens, 1987) recalls the celebrated 'Dambusters' raid of 1943 on the Ruhr. A wall of York stone represents a dam, and a central sloping section in green slate the water rushing through a breach. On either side there are rolls of honour in the same material.

This small, pyramidal brick memorial commemorates those who died constructing the Sumatra Railway while prisoners of war in the Second World War. It stands among a group of memorials to those who died in the Far East at the National Memorial Arboretum, Alrewas, Staffordshire. Nearby is a similar memorial to the more notorious Burma Railway.

to be remembered. War memorials provide one of the most complete records of major events which have shaped Britain and their enduring presence at the heart of communities great and small serves to remind all who pass by of the 'pity of war'.

The recapture of British South Atlantic Territories in 1982 was well covered by the media at the time. One of the enduring images of the Falklands War was the Royal Marine Commando 'yomping' over the rugged terrain. This was captured in memorial form (P. Jackson, 1992) on the seafront at Southsea, Hampshire, next to the Royal Marines' museum.

Long stones and high crosses

Free-standing monuments rely on visibility to attract attention even from a distance and, wherever possible, utilise open spaces and/or high ground. Where these are restricted, as in built-up areas, they are often elevated on plinths and pillars or make use of height and mass in the manner of triumphal Roman arches, Greek columns and Egyptian obelisks. A few employ ancient megalithic forms, either rough-hewn or worked. Memorials located inside buildings rely on their hosts to draw attention to them, as demonstrated most clearly in the case of churches.

Obelisks – uniform square pillars tapering to a pyramidal apex – were associated with important sacred and secular sites, where they were often located at entrances to buildings or temple complexes. Their available flat surfaces invited inscriptions, which often praised powerful people or recorded major events such as victories in war. In Britain they first appeared as decorative motifs in low relief on tombs and some wall monuments in medieval churches. The growth of antiquarianism in the eighteenth century increased their use in decorative and commemorative works while British military success against Napoleon in North Africa increased their popularity. The belated arrival of Cleopatra's Needle in 1878 gave an added incentive for the use of obelisks in public monumentalia, as memorials to the Boer War demonstrate.

This 23 foot sandstone monolith, now protectively encased in glass, commemorates a battle which took place near Forres in Moray in the tenth century. Richly carved with battle scenes, it is believed to commemorate a Picto-Scots victory over invading Danes, possibly led by Sueno, by whose name the stone is usually known.

Believed to be the largest single piece of granite quarried in Britain, this 25 foot monolith forms the basis of the Bedfordshire town of Leighton Buzzard's memorial, set in a square in front of the parish church, whose boundary wall creates the impression of a precinct. It took three days to erect in 1920 and bears the names of those killed in both world wars and of one who fell in the Korean War.

The Egyptian originals were quarried as monoliths, which gave them a magical quality, but modern obelisks are invariably formed from the assembly of man-made sections. When built on a grand scale and also sited in open country or town squares they make impressive landmarks. As mounts for statuary they tend to lose their distinctive character, especially when truncated or beheaded. On occasion they may be 'stepped' in the manner of early pyramids, which is less damaging to their integrity. Their surfaces may be inscribed but it is more common for war memorials to have dedications recorded on the base along with narrative or commemorative plaques.

Unlike obelisks, columns almost invariably consist of an assembly of bases, shafts and capitals. Shafts may be plain, fluted or rostral, and capitals usually conform to one or other of the classical 'orders'. Originally used collectively as roof supports for

The shaft of Plymouth's rose-red polished granite Boer War obelisk was erected close to the famous Hoe. Plaques around the base depict scenes of action, in one of which the death of Queen Victoria's grandson, Charles Victor of Schleswig-Holstein, is shown.

At 100 feet, Blackpool's seafront obelisk of Cornish granite (Prestwich & Sons, 1923) is Britain's tallest. On its base are fine relief panels (Ledward), one of which includes a domestic cat! To either side are war-stones bearing the names of the fallen.

Right: *The focal point of Stivichall War Memorial Park in Coventry is a massive obeliskal tower, on which are superimposed a large cross and the arms of the city. A hall of memory is housed within it, while a perpetual light shines from its top in the manner of a 'lanterne des morts'.*

Left: *At Stourbridge in Worcestershire a polished red granite obelisk has been 'decapitated' to serve as a pedestal for an unusual kneeling Victory bearing banners (Cassidy, 1922). Around the base is a relief panel featuring a military parade, which includes a Mark IV tank and a motorcycle despatch rider.*

Close to the west door of Westminster Abbey in Broad Sanctuary is a 'Gothic' confection. A polished red granite Corinthian column supports a 'lantern', from whose windows assorted monarchs regally gaze while above them St George slays a dragon (Gilbert Scott, 1861). Its purpose was to commemorate former pupils of Westminster School who died in the Crimea and the Indian Mutiny.

major works or as decorative pilasters, their use in free-standing form to mount real or allegorical statuary was developed by the Greeks and extended for primarily triumphal purposes by the Romans. Their use in Britain stems essentially from the classical revival in architecture following the Restoration. The largest versions have always been in a minority, not least because of the high cost of construction. Nelson's monument in Trafalgar Square took years to complete because of the shortfalls in public subscriptions, while that of the 'Grand Old Duke of York' was only financed by stopping one day's pay from all ranks in the Army.

Free-standing or high crosses have long been archetypically British landscape features. If not the direct lineal descendants of pagan 'menhirs', they have certainly inherited their purposive element of veneration for ancestors, nowhere more so than when used as war memorials. Crosses used for this purpose are far more common in Britain than elsewhere. In Celtic areas the tradition of creating them in stone is directly attributable to geography and the introduction of cross-slabs from Ireland before the sixth century. The later use of elaborate carving on the shafts owes much to Viking influence. In Saxon areas the proliferation of crosses, mainly as preaching stations before the advent of permanent parish churches, stems from the Augustine missions begun in the late seventh century. Most were

On land donated by the Guinness family by the side of the main London to Norwich road in Suffolk rises a 127 foot fluted Corinthian column, on top of which is a Greek funerary urn. It commemorates the men of the parishes of Elveden, Eriswell and Icklingham, whose boundaries meet at this point. Forty-eight names are recorded for the First World War and six, including Viscount Elveden, for the Second.

Until the nineteenth century, 'Celtic' wheel-headed crosses were not common in southern Britain, but their deployment in Victorian churchyards and cemeteries knew no bounds. This large roadside example in the New Forest village of Hinton is typical of the many produced by local firms of masons after the First World War.

fashioned in wood and have not survived, although their tradition of gable-headed 'roods', more shrine than cross, was later duplicated in stone for churchyard and cemetery use. Five thousand crosses of many kinds existed in England alone before the Reformation, when most were attacked by iconoclasts. As public religious monumentalia they did not regain primacy until widely used as mementos mori in Victorian cemeteries, strongly influenced by contemporary 'Celtic' and 'Gothic' revivalism in religious art.

Crosses were deployed as corporate churchyard monuments for the anonymous dead of medieval parishes, so that crosses used as war memorials have a close ancestral link to them. They were also used as waymarkers, particularly of lich or 'corpse' roads used to bring the dead for burial in churchyards from outlying areas. Some took on the appearance of shrines on

Below left: The churchyard cross at Ketton in Rutland stands among venerable gravestones, a reminder of its medieval forebears. It is in the form of a pre-Reformation gable-headed rood, of a type originally carved in wood and favoured with destruction by iconoclasts. Ketton stone, once prized for sculpture, is now more commonly used in civil engineering.

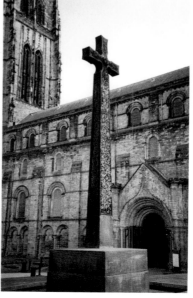

This free-armed, Saxon-headed cross stands within the precincts of Durham Cathedral. Its long shaft is decorated with elaborate strapwork, through which animals and birds can be glimpsed. It is a memorial to men of the Durham Light Infantry who served in the Boer War, 1899–1902.

This unmarked, slender Maltese-headed churchyard cross was re-erected on a pre-Reformation pedestal at St Mary's Church, Teynham, in Kent by the parents of Captain G. Selby, an army doctor, in tribute to him and a nearby First World War Voluntary Aid Detachment hospital. His repatriated battlefield burial cross is inside the church.

pilgrims' ways, giving rise to a uniquely English architectural variety, the Eleanor or 'spire' cross.

The Imperial War Graves Commission instigated a competition to find a monumental form suitable for universal use in its military cemeteries worldwide.

Above: *One of Eric Gill's most idiosyncratic crosses is situated in a large wayside clearing in the hamlet of Briantspuddle, Dorset. On the front is a tall, lugubrious adult Christ; on the reverse Mary suckles her infant son under a shrine-like canopy supported by miniature pillars of Portland 'marble'.*

This peculiarly 'medieval' English Eleanor cross was erected in Hereford to commemorate those of the city and county who fell in the First World War. In form, it follows the style of the originals erected by Edward I to mark each halt by his wife's cortege en route for her burial at Westminster Abbey in 1290. A limited number were erected as memorials for the Boer War and for the First World War.

Just outside the churchyard wall of Beaconsfield's restored fifteenth-century parish church is this 'lanterne des morts' with its 'flame' emitting a perpetual light above a distinctly Anglo-Catholic figure of Christ crucified. It is possible that no play on words was intended by using such a beacon in the memorial for this Buckinghamshire town!

Among the designs exhibited were Lutyens's war-stone (in effect an open-air altar), a *lanterne des morts* (a medieval French concept of a perpetually burning cemetery beacon) and the traditional lichgate (the point where originally the 1549 Order for the Burial of the Dead ordained that the priest should receive a body prior to its interment). In the event, the competition was won by Blomfield's quasi-Gothic Cross of Sacrifice, featuring a crusader's sword reversed, which was the subject of much controversy at the time.

Crosses had also featured prominently in the everyday life of medieval towns and villages. They were erected to indicate the sites for moots (councils) and courts, muster points for both ancient fyrds and

The long-shafted 'Gothic' cross, bearing an inverted Crusader's sword, serves as the standard monument in all Commonwealth (formerly Imperial) War Graves Commission military cemeteries worldwide. This one at North Tidworth on Salisbury Plain recalls that this is a garrison town and that war-wounded were brought to its military hospital in both world wars.

Town crosses were common in medieval Britain; much less so is their appearance as war memorials. This 37 foot 'Gothic' model with heraldic shields around the base (Thorpe, 1921) was chosen by a public meeting in Oxford and is in keeping with its medieval surroundings in St Giles.

modern militias, and the place where official proclamations were to be read to assembled citizens. Most significantly, they marked the places where markets and fairs were legally held, often under charter, the most important occasions in medieval life.

Although Lutyens's war-stone was not selected by the Commission it appears in a surprising number of its cemeteries; Brookwood in Surrey even has two. It can also be found in military sections of civic cemeteries. Originally intended as the centrepiece for the abandoned National War Shrine to have been created in Hyde Park, it resembles the altars that once stood in front of Greco-Roman temples. Like his Cenotaph, it has a non-sectarian appeal – altars being common to many faiths – which commended its adoption for a variety of commemorative works.

After the First World War many villages chose crosses for their memorial. In Kent, Boughton Aluph's rough-hewn 'Latin' version stands at the apex of a large triangular village green with its cricket pavilion and pitch. At the edge of the green is the village inn, but the ancient church is some quarter of a mile distant!

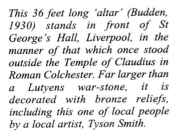

This 36 feet long 'altar' (Budden, 1930) stands in front of St George's Hall, Liverpool, in the manner of that which once stood outside the Temple of Claudius in Roman Colchester. Far larger than a Lutyens war-stone, it is decorated with bronze reliefs, including this one of local people by a local artist, Tyson Smith.

Liminal lights

Although the Romans had introduced the glazing of windows to Britain for practical purposes, it was not until the late seventh century that coloured glass was used to create mosaics in the windows of some Northumbrian churches, probably under Byzantine influence. The use of natural light refracted through coloured or 'pot glass' in this way produced a liminal effect, as if opening a portal between the physical and spiritual worlds. This mystical quality was developed by using stained glass to create pictures of biblical scenes and later to narrate the lives of saints in pictographs. Despite its expense, the use of imported glass was not confined to the churches but these were able to maximise its potential.

The introduction of the medieval 'Gothic' style of architecture made much more window space available for decoration. Tall, vertical panels created 'walls of glass' in which religious and secular themes were pursued. Heraldic symbols and stained glass portraiture of wealthy patrons helped meet the cost of elaborate window art. Most stained glass in England and all of that in Scotland were destroyed by iconoclasts during and after the Reformation. Some windows not overtly 'idolatrous' managed to survive the onslaught and later informed the revival of stained glass work in the nineteenth century.

This group of thirteenth-century medallions set high in the clerestory of the north aisle of the choir in Canterbury Cathedral depicts the siege and capture of the city by the Danes in 1011, following which Archbishop Alphege was murdered. It is the earliest extant window commemorating war in Britain.

Completed in 1357, Gloucester Cathedral's 'Crecy' window, roughly the size of a tennis court, was donated by Lord Thomas Bradeston in memory of his friend Sir Maurice Berkeley, who was killed at Calais in 1347. The bottom row of decoration incorporates the arms of the Black Prince and of knights who fought at Crecy, including those of Berkeley and Bradeston, third and fourth from the right.

Following the Restoration of 1660 the recovery of the art was slow and mainly confined to the painting of pictures on glass with enamels, which failed to match either the luminosity or the liminality of the lost medieval church windows. Destruction and decay caused much old-style glass to be replaced with 'white' (plain) substitutes. Popular amongst the new aristocracy and the commercial classes was heraldry, which was later to provide the platform from which to launch the revival in stained glass. Thomas Willement led the way and as a noted heraldic designer was designated 'artist in stained glass to Queen Victoria', for whom he produced windows in St George's Chapel, Windsor. The great expansion of church building and restoration in the nineteenth century made more window space available for decoration than at any time since the fifteenth century. Families and friends of Britons serving the cause of Empire in distant lands saw the potential of stained glass windows for creating war memorials

The 'Flodden' window in St Leonard's Church, Middleton, Lancashire, shows a company of archers led by Richard Assheton at the eponymous battle against the Scots in 1513. Installed two years after the battle, the window originally comprised three lancets but time and several moves in location have reduced its size and content.

Left: *Most cathedrals and many larger town churches contain regimental chapels replete with books of remembrance and laid-up Colours. Carlisle Cathedral houses the Border Regiment chapel, in which this memorial window was installed early in the twentieth century. It adheres to Victorian medievalism for its main figures but the officer and soldier, their arms reversed, appear in the 'red coats' of late-Victorian pattern.*

Right: *The death of Colonel Durnford when commanding the Natal Native Contingent at Isandhlwana in 1879 is depicted in medieval-style medallions in Rochester Cathedral. The figures who speared him to death appear drawn from a biblical 'host' rather than the Zulu impis actually responsible.*

in a medium which was less expensive than marble and bolder than brass. The new techniques of glass-making and Victorian industrialisation gave rise to windows which caused a reaction against both form and content by the Pre-Raphaelite and the Arts and Crafts movements, whose influences can be detected in memorial windows. Others, such as the younger Pugin, worked to recreate the jewelled effect of medieval windows with their heightened sense of liminality.

Memorial windows produced following the Boer War retain most of the traditional images associated with church glass, but the influence of realism, which is detectable in the developments in 'New Sculpture' of the period, can also be found. Those of the First World War show a predominance of

The figure of David playing a harp below an angel bearing part of the musical score of Handel's 'Largo' suggests a connection with the cathedral choir at Rochester. The memorial is for local men who served with the 15th Battalion, Civil Service Rifles, of the London Regiment in the First World War. The use of 'white' glass helps to give the work a modern feel in ancient surroundings.

Left: This memorial window in St Mary's Church, East Farleigh, Kent, has what is believed to be the earliest figure of a soldier in First World War battledress and a motorised military ambulance. It commemorates Captain Walter of the Royal Flying Corps, whose battlefield cross, formed from the propeller of his crashed biplane, was installed next to the window.

Above left: The figure of St George kneeling in prayer over a slain dragon, from whose throat blood oozes, occupies the twelfth-century west end of the parish church of Allhallows, Hoo, Kent. Although this is a First World War memorial window, below which hangs a local honours board, the style of the work suggests Pre-Raphaelite influences.

Below left: The drama of the evacuation from Dunkirk of the British Expeditionary Force in 1940 is captured in this window full of life in St George's Church, Ramsgate. The small heraldic devices recall the contributions of local people, some of whom are shown below the scenes of evacuation from the beaches.

Left: The contribution of the 59th Surrey (Addington) Battalion Home Guard to local defence during the Second World War is commemorated in Addington parish church. The theme and inscription are biblical but the figures and weaponry suggest Saxon connections. This may be intended to forge a link between the ancient 'fyrd' of Saxon England and the Local Defence Volunteers, redesignated the 'Home Guard' by Churchill.

Right: *The fifty-year association of Swanton Morley in Norfolk with the local RAF station is recalled in this lightly leaded modern window. Below the stylised representation of the Cross of Sacrifice is the station's stag's head emblem; above are silhouettes of aircraft flown from the base between 1940 and 1990.*

Below: *The Nore chapel at St George's Centre, Chatham Maritime, was designed by Edward Maufe, its windows by Hugh Easton. The fifteen lancets in the apsidal-ended chancel commemorate men and women from the manning port who died in the Second World War. The window portraying St Margaret of Antioch slaying a dragon is a tribute to the Women's Royal Naval Service.*

religious and patriotic iconography, as an aid to comforting the bereaved with familiar images, but the process of innovation in stained glass work was not extinguished.

Those created following the Second World War are most notable for their depiction of the 'tumult in the clouds', for which window art was a singularly appropriate medium. Windows depicting the Battle of Britain can be seen to advantage close to epicentres of operation in London and the Home Counties, while many churches in East Anglia particularly recall the close association of their communities with the many bomber squadrons located in their midst. Those reflecting the other armed services are more widely spread, with concentrations in garrison churches and those of the Navy's three manning ports. New forms of glass production and leading techniques have helped widen the scope of memorial windows although their sense of the traditional is still strong.

Most stained glass memorial windows are to be found in cathedrals and major parish churches but secular sites also exist, though in fewer numbers. Schools and colleges,

The Battle of Britain window illuminating the entrance hall of the Rolls-Royce headquarters in Derby is by Hugh Easton. It forges a link between the workers who made the engines for the Spitfires and Hurricanes, and those who flew them to defend Britain and liberate occupied Europe following D-Day in 1944.

This central section of the memorial window which once stood in the Port of London Authority's headquarters in Trinity Square, London, was removed to the Port of Tilbury together with two large ceramic rolls of honour when the PLA was wound up. Their present location means that they are rarely seen. The central figure of Victory is supported by cameos of employees who were killed in the Blitz and members of the rescue services.

Left: The Burma Star Medal presides over an evocative scene for all who fought in the 'Forgotten War', 1941–5. It also bears the famous 'Kohima Epitaph'. It was installed in St John's Church in Cardiff by members of the Burma Star Association.

Below left: Eighteen-year-old air gunner Gunther Anton was shot down over Southampton in 1944 and imprisoned at Houndstone Camp, East Chinnock, in Somerset. Between 1948 and 1982 he made twelve windows at his family's glassworks and gifted them to the church, dying six months later.

Below right: St Nicholas Church, Moreton, in Dorset was all but demolished by a stray bomb intended for a nearby airfield. Replacement windows in etched and engraved glass for the rebuild were made by Laurence Whistler. The beautiful Trinity Chapel window commemorates an anonymous pilot killed soon after his marriage. The ancient Christian 'chi-rho' symbol is shown as a vapour trail in a truly wonderful window.

The early Norman church on Thorney Island in West Sussex originally served a small community which was evacuated before the Second World War to accommodate an RAF station. Its only ornamented window features the lapwing emblem of the station, which operated on Thorney from 1938 to 1976. Through it can be seen war graves in a small military cemetery.

private houses and public buildings, workplaces and recreational areas have all provided locations for commemorative works, their presence all the more effective for being unexpected.

Etched and engraved glass is much less commonly found in window works but where it has been used, especially by a master like Laurence Whistler, it can be striking. It has been used to effect, *inter alia*, in the west screen of Coventry Cathedral, where it divides the new church from the narthex created from its medieval predecessor, whose ruin has been preserved in memorial form, and in the sanctuary window of the Air Forces Memorial at Runnymede in Surrey. It produces the greatest liminality of all window art, its images seeming to float against the natural backgrounds seen 'as through a glass darkly'.

Singularities

All memorials have features which render them unique, no one commemorative work being exactly like another, differentiated by dedication if nothing more. Yet among the commonplace there are those which by virtue of one characteristic or another are atypical among their kind. A simple distinction may, for example, be drawn between those that simply perform the role of remembrance and others with a purposive utilitarian element. The latter include some of the oldest examples of war memorial artefacts and architecture, such as church fabric and furnishing, educational institutions and hospitals. Church bells have been rung for centuries to call worshipers to prayer, to warn of invasion, to celebrate victory and to toll for the dead. Before public clocks were erected in towns and villages bells served to regulate the hours of the day and, with clocks, have been utilised as metaphors for life and death, thus making them singularly appropriate for use in war memorial guise.

While relatively few churches have been built specifically as war memorials, school chapels apart, some like St Clement Danes,

reconstructed after the Blitz in honour of the RAF, have achieved this status, while others, such as garrison churches, have assumed it. It has been estimated that there are some twenty possible classifications for memorial artefacts in churches, too many to consider here in detail. They range from altars, lecterns, pulpits and windows to some of a more unusual description.

Religion and remembrance have an ancient, symbiotic relationship which is reflected in the design of a substantial number of specific instances. Some memorials, notably halls of memory, have been built to resemble places of worship while others employ architectural conventions to create a sense of a place

At Loughborough there stands a 151 foot tower housing a carillon, the first and only one built in Britain as a war memorial. Its bells were cast by Taylor's bell foundry, long established in the town. Regular recitals are played on the carillon, whose tower also houses a military museum on three floors.

Above left: *Herne Bay's 70 foot seafront clocktower was built in 1836, one of the earliest free-standing examples in Britain. Following the Boer War a roll of honour was affixed to the lower north wall. It lists thirty-six names including five members of the St John's Ambulance Brigade. It is believed that all survived the war.*

Above right: *'Trench art' describes a wide range of ephemera produced between 1914 and 1939, a few examples of which became war memorial artefacts. This cross was made from packing cases by men of the Durham Light Infantry and erected at Warlencourt on the Somme to commemorate their comrades who fell there in 1916. Ten years later it was installed in the Regimental Chapel at Durham Cathedral.*

The York and Lancaster Regiment was disbanded in 1968, an event accompanied by the symbolic laying down of arms at Sheffield Cathedral. An unusual screen to the Regimental Chapel was created by the use of swords set in the 'carry' or 'parade' position, opposed by bayonets shown reversed between them.

The memorial to Lawrence of Arabia in St Martin's Church, Wareham, Dorset, emulates a medieval chest-tomb. It was executed in Portland stone by his friend Eric Kennington and finished in 1939. Four years earlier Lawrence had been buried at Moreton. The lettering on the gravestone had been cut by Kennington, who in 1926 had provided illustrations for an edition of Lawrence's 'Seven Pillars of Wisdom'.

Right: *A circular, open colonnade in Cardiff's Alexandra Park forms the basis of the Welsh National Memorial (Comper, 1928). Figures of the 'Sons of Wales' attend the winged figure of the Messenger of Victory (Pegram) at its heart. On the high balustrade there are inscriptions in Welsh by national poets.*

set apart from the generality. Such devices include curtain walls, often curved or even circular, creating raised or sunken precincts, open or closed colonnades and cloisters. Many include rolls of honour on their walls and statuary or other monumentalia, which extends and personalises the commemoration of those to whom they are dedicated.

A belvedere in the form of a diminutive Greek temple at Quarry Park, Shrewsbury, struggles to contain a large statue of St Michael (Wyon, 1922). Usually associated with Air Force memorials, the saint does duty here for the men of Shropshire generally and those of the Shropshire Light Infantry in particular. The father of the sculptor had designed the badge of the Artists' Rifles.

Left: *High on the South Downs above Patcham, Sussex, the Chattri (Henriques, 1921) replicates a temple at cremation sites in India. While Muslims who died while hospitalised in Britain in the First World War were buried at Brookwood military cemetery, Hindus and Sikhs were cremated here. The Royal Pavilion at Brighton had been a military hospital during the war.*

Right: *The Imperial Camel Corps was an ad hoc formation assembled to patrol the Western Desert in the First World War. In the event, it assisted Lawrence in Arabia and helped to capture Jerusalem. The memorial by Cecil Brown, a former Corps officer, installed at the Victoria Embankment Gardens, London, in 1920, commemorated not only those whose deaths are listed on it but also the demise of the Corps.*

Some memorials may be the only extant physical reminders of regiments, ships or squadrons which have been disbanded or subsumed within larger corporate entities. Museums and archive materials apart, memorials are often the only tangible remains of such formations and of those who served in their ranks and followed their colours.

Left: *The First Aid Nursing Yeomanry (FANY), part of the Territorial Force, provided hospital and ambulance staff during the First World War. It survived the post-war reorganisation of the Territorials and in 1933 was redesignated the Women's Transport Corps. In the Second World War more than a third of its strength was allocated to the Special Operations Executive; some of those listed on the memorial at St Paul's Church, Kensington, show the award of George Crosses and Croix de Guerre against their names.*

Fourteen Cyclists' Battalions went to war with the Territorials in 1914. All were to disappear in the post-war reorganisation of the Force. In 1920 the Kent Battalion returned from service in India; thirty years later their memorial in the garrison church at Ferozepore was repatriated and rededicated in Canterbury Cathedral.

Left: *Earl Kitchener of Khartoum, like General Gordon, served at Chatham. While Secretary of State for War he was lost at sea off Orkney, when HMS 'Hampshire', in which he was travelling to Russia, was mined. His equestrian statue, which had stood in Khartoum, the Sudanese capital, was brought to Chatham following the Sudan's independence after the Second World War.*

Below: *This lichgate, built by prisoners of war, once stood in the British cemetery at the infamous Changi jail in Singapore, where many Britons died between 1941 and 1945. It was decided to bring it to Britain in 1972 and erect it at Bassingbourn Barracks. In order to conserve it, it was moved to Alrewas in Staffordshire in 2003, where it now stands amongst other Far East memorials at the National Memorial Arboretum.*

General Gordon astride his camel contemplates passing through the triumphal arch erected at the Royal School of Military Engineering at Brompton, Chatham, to commemorate Royal Engineers who served in the Boer War. Beyond it can be seen the obelisk erected for the First World War and, in the background, the Crimea Gate. The close proximity of these monuments combined with their wide coverage of events is unique among free-standing memorials.

Like its famous predecessor at Bayeux, this centrepiece of the D-Day Museum at Portsmouth is an embroidery not a tapestry. It was created by the Royal School of Needlework and comprises thirty-four panels. Unlike its earlier exemplar, it does not seek to create a continuous narrative of the famous amphibious operation of 1944, but rather a series of cameos. It was installed in the custom-built museum to Operation Overlord in 1984.

Britain's imperial role has been reduced to the direct governance of fragments of its former Empire, in the form of Overseas Territories. Many war memorials erected in lands it once ruled have remained *in situ* but a few have been repatriated, rather as the temporary battlefield crosses of the First World War were in some instances.

There are those memorials which could be classified under a number of heads but which are so uncommon as to warrant individual consideration. Treating them as such is in no way intended either to enhance their standing at the expense of others or to diminish it by comparison.

Monumentalists

During and after the Napoleonic Wars there was great demand for public monumentalia depicting national heroes. This created a trend for most of the nineteenth century, during which the Neoclassical style was paramount. One of its leading exponents was **Sir Richard Westmacott** (1775–1856), the head of a family of sculptors, a one-time student of Canova, and the owner of his own bronze foundry. Neoclassical forms continued to predominate in public works until the First World War but they came under increasing pressure from 'New Sculpture' by the end of the Victorian period. One who bridged both 'schools' was **Adrian Jones** (1845–1938), who became a sculptor after some twenty-three years as an army veterinary officer. His most celebrated work was to be *Peace in Her Quadriga*, erected on top of Decimus Burton's Wellington Arch in London in 1912, the largest bronze sculpture ever cast in Britain. It replaced an over-indulgent equestrian study of the Iron Duke, removed to Aldershot thirty years earlier. While his approach to the new initiatives in sculpture was tentative, others were bolder.

'New Sculpture' was a reaction against what was seen as blandness in public works. To counter this, its supporters advocated the use of 'natural' surface textures and greater animation of the subject matter. Two converts to the cause were **William Goscombe John** (1860–1952), who had studied with Rodin in Paris, and **Albert Toft**

The Royal Dockyard in Chatham closed its gates in 1984 after four centuries of serving the Royal Navy. It became a World Heritage Site, and HMS 'Cavalier', the last-surviving Second World War destroyer, one of several memorials here, now occupies the dock where HMS 'Victory' was built and later refitted to serve as Nelson's flagship at the Battle of Trafalgar. The royal arms (Coade & Sealy, 1812) are above the main gate, first entered by Midshipman Nelson in 1771.

While Adrian Jones is noted for his equestrian figures, this monument in the Mall, London, to the Royal Marines who fell in the China and Boer Wars shows his skills in a wider context. The memorial, whose reliefs of battle (Sir T. Jackson) are almost too lifelike, was refurbished and extended to become the Royal Marines National Memorial in 2000.

(1862–1949), a former Staffordshire potter, both of whom created notable Boer War memorials before adding to their reputation with memorials for the First World War.

The chief propagandist for the movement was **George Frampton** (1860–1928), whose own work attracted criticism but not the same critical acclaim which was accorded to **Charles Sargeant Jagger** (1885–1934), the only one

Left: *Goscombe John is noted for his bronzes, which have been justly acclaimed, but he also worked in stone. This monument at Liverpool's Pierhead was originally intended as a tribute to engine-room staff who died on board the 'Titanic' when it sank in 1912, but it became a tribute to all 'engine-room heroes' of all First World War ships.*

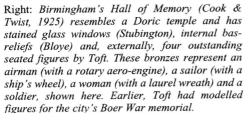

Right: *Birmingham's Hall of Memory (Cook & Twist, 1925) resembles a Doric temple and has stained glass windows (Stubington), internal bas-reliefs (Bloye) and, externally, four outstanding seated figures by Toft. These bronzes represent an airman (with a rotary aero-engine), a sailor (with a ship's wheel), a woman (with a laurel wreath) and a soldier, shown here. Earlier, Toft had modelled figures for the city's Boer War memorial.*

among his contemporaries to have made his reputation almost entirely from his war memorial works. His monument to the Royal Artillery stands adjacent to Jones's *Quadriga* and the Neoclassical but inappropriate figure of David on the Machine Gun Corps monument executed by **F. Derwent Wood** (1871–1926). Jagger's work has been rightly acclaimed as one of the greatest of twentieth-century sculptures.

During the First World War the Imperial War Graves Commission appointed a group of architects and sculptors to create monuments for the British dead and 'missing', and their collaborative works are the nearest approximation to a 'school of war memorialists'. **Edwin Lutyens** (1869–1944) was one of the three principal architects appointed by the Commission, being justly acclaimed for his Cenotaph in London and his Thiepval Gate on the Somme, only two amongst a prodigious output of war memorial projects. Alongside him worked **Reginald Blomfield** (1856–1942), famous for his Menin Gate at Ypres (atop which is a huge lion executed by **William Reid Dick**, 1878–1961, with whom Blomfield collaborated in other projects). Blomfield is credited with the design of the Cross of Sacrifice, used by the Commission in all of its military cemeteries, although the concept originated with the third principal architect, **Herbert Baker** (1862–1946).

The Scots architect **Robert Lorimer** (1864–1929) designed the monuments installed at each of the Navy's

Above: *George Frampton's monument in St Martin's Place, London, to Edith Cavell (1920), who was shot as a spy in Brussels in 1915, was not well received. It was criticised for its 'modernity' of style as well as the pedestrian treatment of its subject. The figure of the martyred nurse in marble is somewhat overpowered by the allegory attempted in the massive pedestal.*

Railway companies across Britain commissioned memorials for their employees killed in the First World War. The choice of Jagger by the Great Western Railway for its monument at Paddington station was inspired, its chosen location was not. This fine work of 'Tommy' dressed for the trenches reading a letter from home deserves better treatment. Jagger won a Military Cross in France, where his work has been prized, but at Paddington 'Tommy' has been shunted into a siding on Platform 1.

Lutyens's cenotaph for Southampton includes all those features he would have liked to have included in the abandoned War Shrine in Hyde Park – a war-stone, fir cones on pylons and a body in a coffin. It was completed a year before his acclaimed work in Whitehall, in which there is no flamboyance.

Right: *Oundle School's free-standing chapel (Blomfield, 1923) in Northamptonshire is a late example of Victorian Gothic Revival. Such chapels are the exception to the general rule that churches are not often created to serve as war memorials per se. Its stained glass by Hugh Easton, who designed the Battle of Britain Memorial window in Westminster Abbey, depicts the Seven Ages of Man, to which more modern window art has been added.*

All the Imperial War Graves Commission monuments to the 'missing' of the Royal Navy (Lorimer, 1927) are similar but no two are identical. The central feature in each is an obelisk-like column sur-mounted by a globe and figures representing the four winds above ships' prows (Poole), which renders the columns rostral. All three were extended after the Second World War (Maufe) and enlivened at ground level by statues at intervals along the precincts' walls (Wheeler). That shown here is on Southsea Common in Portsmouth.

The statue of Albert Ball, awarded a posthumous Victoria Cross in 1916, stands in the castle grounds of his native Nottingham. The figure is in contemporary flying gear and sheltered by a female figure (Poole). Public monuments to those awarded Britain's highest honour for bravery are exceptional.

three manning ports, with sculpture contributed by **Henry Poole** (1873–1928), who managed to reconcile allegory with realism in a number of other works. Lorimer was also commissioned to design the Scottish National War Memorial, for which he employed 'Scots Baronial' architecture to make it blend in with the rather austere surroundings of Edinburgh Castle, within which it stands. After the Second World War the Commonwealth War Graves Commission employed **Edward Maufe** (1883–1974) to extend each of the three Navy monuments and that of the Merchant Marine on Tower Hill in London as well as designing the Air Forces Memorial at Runnymede.

Another major contributor to the style adopted for war memorials was **Eric Gill** (1882–1940), who began his career as a letter cutter on Boer War memorials. He was a wood carver *par excellence* and the reviver of the medieval art of 'direct carving' in stone without resort to the use of a maquette to produce the finished work. He believed in the use of local stone wherever possible, which can be detected in his many idiosyncratic war memorial crosses. He collaborated on occasion with **Jacob Epstein** (1880–1959), whose style was too revolutionary for the great majority of critics. Others who resorted to the method were **Eric Kennington** (1888–1960), who was, like Stanley Spencer, an Official War Artist in both world wars, and **Harold Ledward** (1888–1960), a late convert to the cause.

The Scottish National War Memorial was created in 'Scots Baronial' style (Lorimer, 1927) within the walls of Edinburgh Castle. It houses an elaborate hall of memory and a 'shrine', whose apsidal end, shown here, gives the appearance of a church. Over two hundred artists and craftworkers contributed to its fabric and furnishings. It features memorials to Scots regiments and service personnel, as well as to women's organisations and even animals.

Eric Gill's monument at Chirk in north Wales is usually classified as a diminutive example of an obelisk but, as usual with Gill, nothing is that simple. Instead of being topped with a pyramidal head, it has conjoined gables usually associated with medieval external wooden roods. The figure of a soldier crouched under a greatcoat, although in need of restoration, is pure Gill.

Stanley Spencer (1891–1959) made his reputation as one of the finest exponents of free-form art in the twentieth century. His reputation for war memorial work is almost exclusively confined to the series of paintings he produced for the Sandham Memorial Chapel at Burghclere in Hampshire, designed specifically to hold these works by **Lionel Pearson**, who had collaborated with Jagger on the Royal Artillery Monument. Examples of his work as an Official War Artist are held by the Imperial War Museum, which has in the region of ten thousand pieces produced by many artists in both world wars for the Ministry of Information, not as war memorial works but for public information purposes.

Many sculptors have contributed to war memorials, including the prolific Scot **William Birnie Rhind** and fellow

Below right: *The self-taught sculptor Eric Kennington completed this group based on Kipling's 'Soldiers Three' in Portland stone in 1924. It was installed at Battersea Park in London to commemorate 'Tommies' of the 24th (East Surrey) Infantry Division. Although the monument was influenced by ancient Egyptian architectural figures, some critics found it too modern! The soldier poet Robert Graves was the model for the head of the soldier with the rifle on his shoulder.*

Right: *Stockport's Art Gallery was opened in 1925, the popular choice for a utilitarian war memorial subscribed for by townspeople. Behind its classical façade lies an exhibition space on two floors and a marbled hall of memory rising the height of the building. It houses this impressive group sculpted by Ledward, depicting Britannia shielding a fallen hero and trampling the serpent of war.*

The Oratory Chapel of All Souls at Burghclere in Hampshire was designed by the architect Lionel Pearson, who created the 'Howitzer' base for Jagger's Royal Artillery Monument in London. The chapel was commissioned to commemorate a soldier who, like Stanley Spencer, had served in Macedonia. Between 1927 and 1932 Spencer worked on nineteen canvases, not murals as some have thought. It has been considered one of his finest works.

Scots **Alexander Carrick** and **Kellock Brown**, along with the Irishman **John Cassidy** and the Canadian **R. Tait Mackenzie**. The overwhelming majority of monumental works were created by local firms of stonemasons, some of whose output – like that of **Snell & Company** (Cornwall), **White & Sons** (Birmingham) and **Stewart & Company** (Aberdeen) – supplied customers further afield. The use of wood for external projects has not been much in evidence, save in the construction of lichgates, whereas Ketton, Portland, York, granite and even the artificial Coade stone have been widely used. Modern technology applied to wood preservation has brought about a slow increase in the use of wood for major external projects, examples of which can be seen at the National Memorial Arboretum at Alrewas in Staffordshire.

War memorials include some outstanding works of art amongst

their number but the majority do not aspire to such distinction; like all war memorials, their purpose is to act as remembrancers for past generations who have experienced war in Britain and elsewhere. Artistic interpretation distils sensation and enhances it in memorable form so as to attract the gaze of those who become aware of the physical presence of memorials in their midst.

The life-size figure of a polar bear (Benson, 1998) was the first sculpture installed at the National Memorial Arboretum, Alrewas. It commemorates the 49th (West Yorkshire) Division in the Second World War, a division that was prominent in Arctic campaigns. The badges of each unit in the division are carved in limewood and set around the base behind a protective glass shield.

Further reading

Baker, Margaret. *Discovering London Statues and Monuments*. Shire, fifth edition 2002.

Barnes, Richard. *The Obelisk*. Frontier, 2004.

Beatty, David. *Light Perpetual*. Airlife, 1995.

Beckett, Ian. *Discovering British Regimental Traditions*. Shire, 1999.

Boorman, Derek. *At the Going Down of the Sun: British First World War Memorials*. William Sessions, 1988.

Boorman, Derek. *For Your Tomorrow: Second World War Memorials*. William Sessions, 1995.

Borg, Alan. *War Memorials*. Leo Cooper, 1991.

Brown, Malcolm. *The First World War*. Pan Books, 2002.

Connelly, Mark. *The Great War: Memory and Ritual*. Royal Historical Society, 2002.

Darke, Jo. *The Monument Guide to England and Wales*. MacDonald, 1991.

Farwell, Brian. *The Great Boer War*. Wordsworth Military, 1991.

Farwell, Brian. *Queen Victoria's Little Wars*. Wordsworth Military, 1999.

Foster, Mark. *The World at War*. Pimlico, 2001.

Gibbons, Edwin, *et al. Courage Remembered*. The Stationery Office Books, 1989.

Harris, Michael. *The War Artists*. London, 1983.

Imperial War Museum. *The War Memorials Handbook*. United Kingdom National Inventory of War Memorials, 2001.

Kernot, Charles. *British Public School War Memorials*. London, 1927.

King, Alex. *Memorials of the Great War in Britain*. Oxford, 1998.

Longwith, Peter. *The Unending Vigil: War Graves 1917–1967*. Commonwealth War Graves Commission, 1968.

McIntyre, Charles. *Monuments of War: How to Read War Memorials*. Robert Hale, 1990.

Saunders, David. *British Maritime Memorials and Mementoes*. Stephens, 1996.

Smith, David. *British Aviation Memorials and Mementoes*. Stephens, 1992.

War Memorials Trust. *Bulletin*. London, quarterly.

Whittock, Arnold. *War Memorials*. London, 1946.

Kathleen Scott's 'Thinking Soldier' perhaps recalled the artist's time spent as a student of Rodin in Paris before her marriage to Captain Scott of Antarctic fame. Huntingdon's memorial was gifted to the town by the local Federation of Women's Institutes in 1923. Among the dedications was one to the Huntingdon Cyclist Battalion, which was revived in the Second World War as a Home Guard unit.

The largest war cemetery in Britain was opened in 1917 at Brookwood in Surrey by the Imperial War Graves Commission and is maintained by its Commonwealth successor. In addition to some five thousand graves, there are several monuments, including this one dedicated to nearly 3500 men and women of HM Land Forces who were lost at sea or in occupied Europe during the Second World War and who have no known grave.

Gazetteer

Only a small cross-section of sites from among the thousands across Britain can be highlighted here. The largest concentrations of war memorial subjects are to be found in the cities and larger towns but churches everywhere have usually more than one example of the twenty or so categories of commemoration which have been identified with places of worship. The sites listed are not intended to be definitive but to encourage further inquiry into the nature and contribution of war memorials to local and national history.

ENGLAND
Bedfordshire
Bedford. In the Embankment Gardens the stone figure of Justice Triumphant (Jagger) represents a departure by the sculptor from the bronze 'Tommies' for which he is justly celebrated.

Kempston. The Greco-Egyptian memorial of the Bedfordshire Regiment on a main-road site opens on to a garden of remembrance.

Leighton Buzzard. The rough-hewn monolith has pride of place in an old square next to the parish church.

Luton. A bronze female figure of Victory (Thornycroft/Blomfield) occupies a prime town-centre position.

Berkshire
Crowthorne. Wellington College Memorial Chapel has a white marble figure of St George on a black marble pedestal (Lutyens).

Pangbourne. The former Nautical College has a Falklands Memorial Chapel.

Reading. The University campus at Whiteknights has a Memorial Clocktower, while the Maiwand Lion continues to roar defiance in Forbury Gardens.

Buckinghamshire

Amersham. The Memorial Cross backed by a later retaining wall stands in a town-centre garden of remembrance.

Beaconsfield. The *lanterne des morts* shares its perpetual light with the adjacent parish churchyard.

Chesham. A solitary 'Tommy' rests on his rifle, butt grounded, on a plinth in a paved area of the town square.

High Wycombe. Wycombe Air Park with memorials and memorabilia now occupies the former RAF pilot training school.

Cambridgeshire

Cambridge. Most colleges have memorials to their alumni. The civic memorial, featuring a homing 'Tommy', stands south of the city centre in Hills Road.

Ely Cathedral. Stained glass centre of excellence.

Trumpington. An idiosyncratic wayside cross, one of whose four relief panels has a demonstrably feminine dragon being slain by St George (Gill).

Wisbech. A large Celtic cross and wall of remembrance in a town-centre garden setting.

Cheshire

Birkenhead. A huge stone catafalque dominates other, smaller memorials in Hamilton Square.

Chester Cathedral. Naval and military memorials.

Crewe. Despite urban development plans, Britannia (Gilbert) still presides over the town square.

Hoylake and West Kirby. An early, heroic 'Tommy' (Jagger) guards the obelisk.

Port Sunlight. The centrepiece cross has a remarkable tableau of military and civilian sculpture (Goscombe John), a masterwork.

Stalybridge. On one side of the approach to the river crossing a dying soldier is protected by an angel; the same service is provided to a sailor on the other (Blundstone).

Stockport. A utilitarian art gallery shares a classically inspired building with a hall of memory.

Cornwall

Bodmin. 'Tommy', grenade in hand, stands in front of the county regiment's museum.

Bude. A flaming oil lamp tops the local variation of the cenotaph theme.

Newquay. High above the town on the headland a cross tops a large cairn.

Penzance. The stones forming the obelisk are dovetailed and pinned with bronze nails to withstand local weather conditions.

Sennen. A Cornish version of the wheel-head cross stands in the churchyard, the closest memorial to Land's End.

Truro. In sight of the cathedral a jubilant 'Tommy', rifle in hand, flourishes his helmet aloft.

Cumbria

Carlisle. The cathedral houses the regimental chapel of the Border Regiment and its rolls of honour.

Great Gable. A stone commemorating members of the Fell and Rock Climbing Club of Great Britain stands near the 3000 foot summit of the mountain.

Kendal. 'Tommy', with rifle slung, gazes around the Market Square.

Keswick. Victory, in relief on a Roman-inspired cemetery stele, watches the northern approach to the town.

Penrith. The shaft of the cross at Eamont Bridge bears bronze reliefs of two Boer War soldiers.

Derbyshire

Alfreton. A soldier protects a young child (Aumonier).

Chesterfield. At Brimington, Victory (Jagger), an allegorical departure from the artist's norm.

Crich. A large, hilltop *lanterne des morts*, nicknamed 'The Lighthouse', commemorates men of the Sherwood Foresters.

Derby. A widowed mother and her child are posed in front of a large Celtic cross (Walker) in the old Market Place; near the former Midland railway station a cenotaph flanked by two obelisks (Lutyens) serves as the memorial for the company's employees; in the Rolls-Royce Head Office building is the fine window depicting the link between the factory's workers and RAF pilots (Easton).

Quarndon. A replica of an Iona cross stands tall in the churchyard.

Devon

Crediton. A unique memorial in the form of a roofed market cross.

Exeter. The cathedral has memorials to the County Regiment; a large Victory presides over the civic memorial in Northernhay Park; the Phoenix fountain's reliefs depict the bombing of the city in 1942.

Plymouth. The historic Hoe and its environs are the focal point for several imposing memorials – the Boer War obelisk; Royal Marine, Royal Navy and 'Armada' monuments; the International Air Monument (Pamela Taylor); a bronze figure of Victory (Birnie Rhind) in a granite-girt precinct. The Guildhall has a fine window depicting devastating air raids on the city, an event also recalled by the partially restored King Charles Church.

Torquay. A cenotaph (Blomfield) occupies pride of place in Princess Gardens.

Dorset

Bournemouth. A massive masonry block surrounded by a confection of columns and urns enclosed by a balustraded terrace in Upper Pleasure Gardens.

Briantspuddle. A very distinctive wayside cross/shrine (Gill).

Corfe Castle. The stone-roofed 'Tudor' arch giving entrance to the village cemetery is in fact a war memorial.

Lyme Regis. A war-stone and large ship's anchor in George Square Gardens were installed as late as 1992 through the efforts of the local British Legion branch.

Moreton. The church of St Nicholas has a unique collection of engraved windows and in the cemetery the grave of Lawrence of Arabia.

Osmington. On the bus route from Weymouth to Wareham, the memorial is a thatched bus shelter.

Wareham. Lawrence, in Arab dress, lies on his 'tomb' in St Martin's Church.

Durham

Bishop Auckland. A cross tops a catafalque in the Market Place.

Darlington.The War Memorial Hospital has a commemorative obelisk in its forecourt.

Durham Cathedral has the Warlencourt cross inside and the Saxon-headed Boer War cross in the Close.

Gateshead has a massive catafalque in a precinct close to the town's art gallery.

South Shields. A remarkable bronze figure of a helmsman at the wheel of his ship at Mill Dam commemorates all mariners who sailed from the port in the Second World War.

Essex

Chelmsford. The cathedral monuments and windows reflect the presence of many local airfields during the Second World War.

Colchester. A large bronze Victory supported by St George at the base of the monument (Fehr) stands in front of the Castle Museum, which holds the stele of Flavius Facilis, probably the earliest surviving war memorial artefact in Britain, dated c.AD 50.

East Tilbury. A flaming lamp within a stone arch in the local park commemorates employees of the Bata Shoe Company.

Southend-on-Sea. A slender obelisk (Lutyens).

Walton on the Naze. A pillar bearing the RAF badge on top and supported by propeller blades from a Halifax bomber stands in the churchyard.

Gloucestershire

Bream. A large cenotaph belies the smallness of the local community in this Forest of Dean village.

Bristol. Denied a site on College Green by the cathedral authorities, an unimpressive cenotaph was erected in Colston Avenue.

Cheltenham. A Boer War obelisk is rather less grand than the cloisters of the College as a war memorial.

Gloucester. The cathedral has the magnificent Crecy Window, a diminutive cross carved by Colonel Carne, VC, while he was a prisoner of war in Korea, and a large 'medieval' war memorial cross in the Close. Nearby, the City burgesses decided to add a curved wall of remembrance to the existing sphinx-topped pylon of the Gloucestershire Regiment erected in 1933!

Hampshire

Aldershot. Exiled from his arch at Hyde Park, the equestrian figure of the Duke of Wellington sits, massively, in solitary state on Round Hill.

Burghclere. The Sandham Oratory Chapel holds the remarkable collection of paintings depicting war in the Balkans in the First World War (Spencer).

Portsmouth. A perambulation along the seafront from the Naval Dockyard to Eastney Barracks is a time trail of monuments from Trafalgar to the Falklands, taking in the Garrison church and the D-Day Museum. Not far away are other memorials in the Guildhall Precinct, with its cenotaph and wall of remembrance guarded by naval and military machine gunners (Jagger). A gate leads to more monuments in Victoria Park.

Southampton. The notable and embellished cenotaph (Lutyens) is in West Park. The bombed church of Holyrood has been preserved as a memorial to the Merchant Marine services.

Herefordshire

Goodrich Castle has windows commemorating the work of radar research and operation locally during the Second World War.

Hereford. The cathedral holds many of the local memorials but the Eleanor cross in St Peter's Square is among the few examples of this type of war memorial.

Walford. A column and attendant figures in the village were restored in 2003 with the help of the War Memorials Trust.

Hertfordshire
Bishop's Stortford. A renovated obelisk commemorates those killed in the First World War.

Bushey. The classical figure of a female mourner stands on the main road into the town.

Royston. 'Tommy' is depicted among a tableau of his predecessors in period costume with a crow, the town's symbol, at his feet in a memorial recessed into the wall of the park.

St Albans. A high cross stands in the gardens of St Peter's Green and a few First World War 'Street Memorials' have been preserved in the town.

Huntingdonshire
Huntingdon. 'The Thinking Soldier' sits centre stage in the main town square in front of the parish church, close to whose wall is a *lanterne des morts*, a Boer War memorial.

Norman Cross. A column bearing an Imperial Eagle marks the location of what was once a camp for Napoleonic prisoners of war.

Ramsey. A memorial chapel was dedicated after the safe return of Lord Ramsey from a prison camp in the Far East after the Second World War.

Warboys. A window dedicated to 'Pathfinders' in the church of St Mary Magdalene commands attention.

Isle of Wight
Arreton. The church has a fine three-light window installed by the Burma Star Association.

Lake has a memorial which incorporates a drinking trough in memory of dogs and horses of the First World War.

Sandown. A quasi-Gothic high cross imposes its substantial presence on the seafront.

Kent
Biggin Hill. St George's Church was built to commemorate the Battle of Britain and has notable windows.

Canterbury. The cathedral has many memorials, including that of the Black Prince. The Saxon-headed hybrid cross stands in the Buttermarket in front of Christ Church Gate. In Dane John Gardens is a fine Boer War monument while in the High Street that of the East Kent Yeomanry incorporates a rare memorial horse trough for the same war.

Capel le Ferne. The Battle of Britain Memorial opened here in 1993.

Dover. The old Marine station has an outstanding bronze group (King) paying tribute to employees of the South Eastern & Chatham Railway Company. The figure of Youth holding a cross aloft stands next to the Library. A memorial to the 60th Rifles' service during the Indian Mutiny is close to the Esplanade in Cambridge Square. Other memorials are associated with the castle above the town.

Maidstone. All Saints Church has several notable memorials dating back to 1795.

Manston. The Spitfire and Hurricane museum is located on the former RAF airfield.

Margate. There is a group of memorials, including the town monument, in Trinity Square and at the Old Town Hall building.

Medway Towns. The Historic Dockyard in Chatham has pride of place but there are significant memorials at the Royal School of Military Engineering, Brompton, and in Rochester Cathedral.

Newnham. The De Laune Cycling Club's unique tribute to its members.

Ramsgate. St George's Church has a large collection of wall monuments and memorial windows.

Lancashire

Accrington. A large obelisk on a massive plinth.

Blackpool. The 100 foot obelisk with relief plaques is the tallest in Britain.

Bolton. A notable Artillery arch in Nelson Square.

Burnley. An outstanding monolithic stone sculptural group with bronze supporters, in Townley Park.

Bury. A prototype figure of a jubilant Boer War soldier, hat raised in salutation (Frampton), and a slender obelisk memorial for the Lancashire Fusiliers (Lutyens), in which regiment the designer's father served.

Lancaster. An imposing figure of Victory set against a wall of memory in Dalton Square.

Liverpool. *The Death of Nelson* (Sir R. Westmacott) at the Exchange Building is a magnificent work. The giant-sized 'altar' stone in front of St George's Hall is unique. Around the Pierhead there is a group of maritime memorials. The King's Regiment Boer War Memorial is elaborately sculpted (Goscombe John).

Manchester. The Boer War memorial (Thornycroft) shows a soldier protecting his fallen comrade. The cenotaph (Lutyens) in St Peter's Square has its coffined body atop the pylon, as at Southampton. Bronze figure of 'Tommy' on sentry duty (Jagger), Britannia Hotel, Portland Street.

Oldham. The 'Tommies' are grouped suggesting a symbolic Calvary.

Preston. The Boer War memorial was removed to Avenham Park to accommodate the massive 70 foot cenotaph (Scott/Pegram) in Market Square.

Southport. The obelisk in the town centre is flanked by open colonnades.

Wigan. The Eleanor cross (Scott) in Hallgate is one of a small number of such memorial forms in Britain.

Leicestershire

Leicester. The impressive Arch of Remembrance (Lutyens) was located in Victoria Park. The Leicester Yeomanry monument stands on high ground in Bradgate Park, north of the city. The cathedral is adjacent to the High Street.

Loughborough. The carillon in Queen's Park has forty-seven working bells.

Melton Mowbray. The Memorial Hospital, now redundant, is Grade II listed.

Lincolnshire

Lincoln. The memorials at the cathedral reflect the number of Air Force bases associated with the county. The civic monument is a large, lantern-head cross in St Benedict's Square.

Waddington. The memorial clock is supported by what appears to be a lamp-post.

Woodhall Spa. There is a Wellington column and the 'Dambusters' memorial at the main crossroads.

London and Middlesex

Many memorials and monuments are concentrated in central London and the following are perambulations designed to take in the majority of those most accessible.

1. *Parliament Square to Hyde Park.* Broad Sanctuary – Westminster Abbey, Westminster School column. Victoria Street – Westminster Cathedral (St Patrick's Chapel). Hobart Place – Rifle Brigade memorial (Tweed). Grosvenor Place, Hyde Park Corner – Constitution Arch (Burton), Machine Gun Corps (Derwent Wood), Duke of Wellington on Copenhagen (Boehm), Royal Artillery Monument (Jagger). Hyde Park – Achilles (Westmacott), Cavalry Monument (A. Jones).

The obelisk-like column topped by an orb in the grounds of the Royal Hospital, Chelsea, commemorates the 255 officers and men of the 24th Regiment named on the column who fell at Chillianwalla during the Second Sikh War in 1849. The 24th Regiment is incorporated within the Royal Regiment of Wales.

2. *Hyde Park Corner to Parliament Square.* Constitution Hill – Commonwealth Forces Gateway. The Mall – Royal Artillery Boer War, Royal Marines Monument. Waterloo Place, Lower Regent Street – Guards Crimea Monument. St James's Park – Royal Naval Division Fountain (Lutyens), Guards Division Monument (Ledward). Whitehall – Royal Tank Regiment (Mallock), Gurkha Monument (Jackson), Earl Haig (A. Jones), Field Marshals Slim, Alanbrook and Montgomery, Cenotaph (Lutyens).

3. *Parliament Square to Wilton Place.* Millbank, Chelsea Bridge – Dragoon Guards Boer War (A. Jones). Chelsea Bridge, Battersea Park – East Surrey Division memorial (Kennington) and ANZAC memorials. Albert Bridge, Royal Hospital Road – National Army Museum, Royal Hospital. Sloane Street, Sloane Square – Men of Chelsea Cross of Sacrifice (Blomfield). Cliveden Place, Eaton Square, Wilton Street – First Aid Nursing Yeomanry memorial and St Paul's School Memorial, St Paul's Church.

4. *Parliament Square to Southwark Cathedral.* Thames Embankment – Chindit memorial, RAF Monument (Blomfield/Reid Dick), Fleet Air Arm (Butler), General Gordon (Hamo Thornycroft), General Outram (Noble). Victoria Embankment – Imperial Camel Corps (Brown), Belgian Memorial (Blomfield), Submariners First World War memorial (Hatch/Tennyson). Southwark Bridge, Borough High Street – 'Tommy' trudging through mud (Lindsey Clark), Hopmen of London wall plaque, Southwark Cathedral.

5. *Trafalgar Square to St Paul's Cathedral.* St Martin's Lane – Edith Cavell monument (Frampton). Strand – St Clement Danes RAF Church. Bow Street, Great Queen Street - Freemasons' Hall. Kingsway, High Holborn – Pearl Assurance St George (Frampton), Prudential Insurance Memorial, Royal Fusiliers City of London Regiment (Toft). Newgate Street, Cheapside, Poultry, Royal Exchange – Wellington (Chantry), Bank of England Memorial, London Troops Monument (Webb/Drury). Queen Victoria Street, Sermon Lane – National Firefighters Memorial. St Paul's Cathedral.

Norfolk
Cromer. Unusual combination of Crucifixion and St George slaying a dragon.
Great Yarmouth. An obelisk on a massive base (First World War) with a wall of remembrance (Second World War) in a garden setting. Far East Prisoners of War Clocktower, seafront. Britannia column.
Norwich. Cathedral with Erpingham Gate Agincourt contemporary monument. Cenotaph (Lutyens) next to City Hall. Cavell memorial bust on plinth (Pegram) at Tombland. Boer War memorial (Toft), Agricultural Plain.

Northamptonshire
Kettering. Cenotaph, Dalkeith Place.
Naseby. Lion couchant on small plinth.
Northampton. Stone of Remembrance flanked by obelisks (Lutyens) and Edgar Mobbs Memorial, Abington Square.
Oundle. Town Square obelisk and outstanding School Memorial Chapel (Blomfield).

Northumberland
Alnwick. *Lanterne des morts* with trio of mourning 'Tommies' at base.
Bellingham. Boer War monument incorporating a drinking fountain.
Berwick upon Tweed. Angel of Peace (Carrick).
Blaydon. 'Tommy' in his greatcoat guards the local cemetery.
Newcastle upon Tyne. St George slays a dragon for the Northumberland Fusiliers while local citizens 'Respond' to Kitchener's 'Call', Eldon Square. A winged figure of Victory commemorates the Boer War.

Nottinghamshire
East Markham. Classical 'broken' column symbolising lives cut short.
Newark. Cross of sacrifice.
Nottingham. A 46 feet high triple-arch gate flanked by 250 foot span of curved walling on a site donated by Jesse Boot on Victoria Embankment. Boer War obelisk. Albert Ball, VC, monument, Castle gardens. Crimean War memorial in the form of a Chinese temple at the Arboretum.
Southwell Cathedral has Air Force memorials.

Oxfordshire
Oxford. Individual college memorials. 'Medieval' town cross, St Giles.
Woodstock. Triumphal arch and massive column topped by a figure of the Duke of Marlborough at Blenheim Palace.
Rutland
Cottesmore. Air Force Chapel, St Nicholas Church. Military (RAF) cemetery.
Ketton. Gable-headed churchyard cross in Ketton stone.

Uppingham. Free-standing School Memorial Chapel.

Shropshire
Bridgnorth. 'Tommy' points the way (A. Jones), castle grounds on a high bluff overlooking
the river Severn.
Craven Arms. Idiosyncratic 'Tommy' supported by a dolphin!
Shrewsbury. Volunteer and Yeomanry Boer War 'Tommy', St Chad's Place. St Michael
occupies a diminutive 'temple' belvedere in Quarry Park.

Somerset
Bath. Cross of sacrifice with semicircular wall of remembrance guarded by lions, Victoria
Park.
Bridgwater. Large female 'Civilisation' statue (Angel). Figure of Admiral Blake,
Cromwellian commander.
Burnham-on-Sea. Memorial Hospital and commemorative stone.
East Chinnock. Church of the Blessed Virgin Mary, outstanding collection of modern
stained glass windows.
Mells. Horner family chapel, equestrian figure (Munnings) on plinth (Lutyens) in St
Andrew's Church. Wall monument with wreath (Lutyens) and lettering (Gill).
Weston-super-Mare. Figure of Angel of Peace and wall of remembrance in Grove Park.
Westonzoyland. Monument to last battle on English soil, Sedgemoor.
Yeovilton. Fleet Air Arm Memorial Chapel at active air base.

Staffordshire
Alrewas. National Memorial Arboretum.
Burslem. Stone pylon with 'Tommy' carved in relief and small lectern memorial with
plaque to local recipient of the Victoria Cross, killed at Arnhem.

The statue of a seventeen-year-old Northumberland Fusilier executed by firing squad at Ypres in 1915 (de Comyn, 2000) stands among a semicircle of saplings, one for each man executed in the First World War. The names of some have been added to local war memorials in the early twenty-first century. It is one of a number of modern memorials in the 150 acres of the National Memorial Arboretum in Staffordshire.

Burton upon Trent. Large figure of winged Victory with allegorical attendants below (Fehr).

Lichfield. Cathedral with Zulu screen to Staffords' Chapel.

Stafford. 'Tommy' flourishes his hat aloft in the Market Place.

Wolverhampton. Large, highly stylised red sandstone obelisk next to St Peter's Church.

Suffolk

Bury St Edmunds. Boer War 'Tommy' sits on a diminutive *kopje* or hill.

Elveden. A massive column by the main London–Norwich road dominates the landscape.

Felixstowe. An elegant Corinthian column supports a diminutive Dove of Peace resembling a seagull!

Ipswich. Archetypical mourning 'Tommy' (Toft) tops the Boer War memorial and at the cenotaph, also in Christchurch Park, an unusual assembly of decorative weapons and soldier's field equipment.

Surrey

Chertsey. Jubilant 'Tommy' flourishes his helmet.

Croydon. Cenotaph with supporting figures outside central library and museum. RAF memorial by Purley Way.

Guildford. Raised colonnade with urns and swords of honour. Cathedral has stained glass memorials and book of remembrance for the Surrey Yeomanry.

Reigate and Redhill. Bronze figure carrying small child and caught by brambles (Goulden) signifying 'Mankind's Struggle'.

Runnymede. Air Forces Memorial, the most impressive Second World War monument in Britain.

Woking. Extensive Commonwealth War Graves Commission cemetery, opened in 1917 and replete with monuments.

Sussex

Brighton. Sussex Regiment and civic monument, with water feature, at Old Steine. Fine Boer War 'Bugler', Regency Square. Indian Army Hospital memorial gate at Royal Pavilion.

Eastbourne. Large figure of Victory (Fehr).

Hove. St George (A. Jones) on top of column.

Lewes. Winged figure of Victory.

Patcham. The Chattri monument at crematorium site on the Downs.

Peacehaven. Memorial clocktower.

Worthing. Bronze figure of exultant 'Tommy'. Memorial birdbath in Beach House Park commemorating Second World War carrier pigeons.

Warwickshire

Birmingham. St Martin's Church shares pride of place with Nelson in the redesigned Bull Ring. Boer War Artillery memorial (Toft), Bath Row. Hall of Memory, Broad Street.

Coventry. Ruined medieval St Michael's Cathedral and cross of embers and nails. Large civic obeliskal monument in Stivichall Memorial Park.

Leamington Spa. Mourning 'Tommy' (Toft), Euston Square.

Meriden. National Cyclists' war memorial, an obelisk on village green.

Warwick. Tall, elegant spire cross, Church Street.

Wiltshire

Fovant. Military badges carved into the chalk hillside during both world wars.

North Tidworth. Military cemetery originally catering for nearby Garrison Hospital.

Salisbury. Cathedral. Curved wall of remembrance lit by 'flame' lamps behind ornamental wrought-iron fence in Guildhall Square.

Swindon. Large cenotaph with recessed cross motif in crowded town centre.

Trowbridge. Mourning 'Tommy' (Bantham).

Worcestershire

Bromsgrove. Burma Star column and slate plaques.

Evesham. Curved, stepped wall of remembrance with 'Tommy', rifle slung (Poole), on a tall plinth.

Kidderminster. Severn Valley Railway station, plaque and locomotive 48773 dedicated to Second World War railwaymen of the Corps of Royal Engineers.

Stourbridge. Obelisk topped by Victory bestowing laurel wreath (Cassidy) in The Parks.

Worcester. County Memorial 'Gothic' cross on stepped base in the Cathedral Close, paired with window inside the building.

Yorkshire

Beverley Minster. Soldiers' Chapel.

Bradford. Cenotaph with superimposed cross and military 'guard' figures, Victoria Square.

Halifax. Town-centre cenotaph (White & Sons).

Harrogate. 75 foot obelisk (Prestwich & Company) with bronze reliefs (Ledward).

Huddersfield. 60 foot Victory column on elevated position with open colonnades to the sides in Greenhead Park.

Hull. Second World War cenotaph behind 'heroic' Boer War memorial in Paragon Square.

Keighley. Victory on a tall plinth guarded by excellent bronzes of 'Tommy' and 'Jack'.

Leeds. Remarkable carved stone of 'Christ Expelling the Money Changers from the Temple' (Gill), once the maquette for a huge bronze commissioned by London County Council, now in the University.

Middlesbrough. Cenotaph and wall of remembrance formed by the boundary wall of Albert Park.

Richmond. Elevated Celtic cross memorial to the Green Howards at Frenchgate.

Ripon. Bronze bust of 'Tommy' on obeliskal pillar in Memorial Garden of the cathedral.

Scarborough. 75 foot obelisk on Oliver's Mount, 500 feet above sea level.

Sheffield. Sword screen to York and Lancaster Regimental Chapel in the cathedral, in front of which rises a 90 foot steel mast attended by mourning 'Tommies'. Fine Military Monument to the local regiment in Western Park.

Skipton. Winged bronze of Victory mounted on an obelisk with a figure of Humanity (Cassidy) at the base, Castle Approach.

Sledmere. Remarkable 'Wagoner' Monument to local horse transport unit and nearby probably the finest Eleanor cross memorial, replete with 'medieval' brasses, in Britain.

York. Obelisk and war-stone (Lutyens) commemorating employees of the North Eastern Railway, close to the station. Boer War Eleanor cross (Gilbert Scott) in Dunscombe Place.

SCOTLAND

Aberdeen. A stone lion on a plinth (Macmillan) guards an extension to the art gallery in Union Terrace Gardens, which houses a hall of remembrance.

Aberfeldy, Perth & Kinross. Black Watch Memorial.

Alloa, Clackmannanshire. A kneeling stone figure of a female mourner tops a granite plinth at Tillicoultry, which bears mostly the names of Argyll & Sutherland Highlanders.

Ardrossan, North Ayrshire. Celtic cross with unlikely assemblage of 'Scottish Heroes' on the shaft.

Ayr, South Ayrshire. Royal Scots Fusilier in Second World War battledress.

Birsay, Orkney. Kitchener's Tower at Marwick Head commemorates the sinking of HMS *Hampshire* en route for Russia in 1916.

Blairgowrie, Perth & Kinross. Stone pillar with two mourning 'Jocks' in bronze (Carrick).

Campbeltown, Argyll & Bute. Unusual combination of cenotaph, cross and obelisk rolled into one memorial.

Dingwall, Highland. 'Jock' with fixed bayonet, on guard (Stephenson).

Dornoch, Highland. 'Jock', shielding his eyes, gazes out to sea (Carrick).

Dumfries. A mourning bronze figure of 'Jock' in King's Own Scottish Borderers uniform tops an elaborate pedestal with Greek pillars. There are a number of similar figures in nearby towns and villages: Annan – with fixed bayonet (Price); Maxwelltown – in granite, arms raised in supplication (Price); Penpont – in mourning (Kellock Brown).

Dunbar, East Lothian. Fine modern stained glass windows (Shona McInnes) replacing those lost when the parish church burned down in 1987.

Dundee. Massive stone pylon topped by a signal brazier on the 570 foot Law headland. Black Watch Second World War bronze (Sutherland) at Powrie Brae on the Forfar road.

Edinburgh. Scottish National War Memorial, Edinburgh Castle. Notable bronzes (Carrick) and windows (Strachan), memorials to the twelve Scottish regiments, Women's Services and animals, including canaries, mice and carrier pigeons. Boer War memorials – Black Watch in Market Street and King's Own Scottish Borderers on North Bridge. 'The Call' and Scots Greys' memorials in Princes Street Gardens. National Monument and Nelson's 'Spyglass' on Calton Hill. St Giles Cathedral. Scottish Rugby Football Union Memorial Arch, Murrayfield. Heart of Midlothian Football Club miniature tower and clock, Haymarket. Fettes School statue of 'The Dying Hero' (Birnie Rhind).

Forres, Moray. Sueno's Stone, Nelson's Tower.

Fraserburgh, Aberdeenshire. A seated bronze figure of Peace guarded by an armoured warrior on a tall plinth (Carrick).

Galashiels, Scottish Borders. Equestrian statue (Clapperton) in front of massive clocktower bearing rolls of honour.

Glasgow. St Mungo's Cathedral. Cenotaph, George Square. Equestrian figure of Wellington with fine descriptive bronze plaques of 'Jock' going to the French Wars, Exchange Square. Railway rolls of honour, Central station. Highland Light Infantry Boer War (Birnie Rhind), Cameronians First World War (Lindsey Clark), Kelvinside Park.

Glenfinnan, Highland. 'Jock' in mourning is overawed by the nearby tall tower topped by a 'Clansman', on the spot where Prince Charles Edward Stuart raised his standard in 1745.

Greenock, Inverclyde. Free French Naval memorial, Lyle Hill. Unusual rostral obelisk with 'Celtic' decoration, Memorial Park.

Halkirk, Highland. A grieving mother in highland dress carries a small child.

Hawick, Scottish Borders. Large rectangular high pillar with bronze 'angel' in exceptional gardens next to the town museum.

Inveraray, Argyll & Bute. 'Jock' in Highland uniform, at ease (Kellock Brown), at edge of Loch Fyne.

Inverness, Highland. Nineteenth-century Cameron Highlanders monument in station forecourt. 20 foot 'Cairn of the Dead' on Drummossie Moor commemorates the last battle

High on a hill overlooking the Clyde at Greenock is this melding of the Cross of Lorraine, the symbol of the Free French in the Second World War, and an anchor. The latter recalls their contribution to the War of the Atlantic, 1939–43, longest campaign of the Second World War, and the place of embarkation for many lost at sea.

on British soil, Culloden, 1746.

Iona, Argyll & Bute. Small Celtic cross on seashore near ferry terminal.

Jedburgh, Scottish Borders. A large stone pillar at the head of a flight of stairs close to the ancient abbey grounds.

Kelso, Scottish Borders. A large stone cross.

Kirkcaldy, Fife. A museum and art gallery in a memorial park.

Kirkcudbright, Dumfries & Galloway. A massive ancient warrior in bronze, sword in hand (Paulin), is seated on a pile of rocks at Maclellan's Castle.

Mull, Argyll & Bute. Monolith in small precinct on the hillside overlooking the harbour at Tobermory.

Nairn, Highland. Unusual fluted column, lacking the usual figure atop its capital.

Oban, Argyll & Bute. Two 'Jocks' carry a wounded comrade (Carrick).

Paisley, Renfrewshire. Large bronze of armoured knight on horseback attended by four First World War 'Jocks' (Alice Meredith-Williams).

Portsoy, Aberdeenshire. A granite 'Jock' in the uniform of a Gordon Highlander.

Spean Bridge, Highland. The trio of commandos recalls Kennington/Gleichen First World War models.

Stirling. Castle and Wallace Monument.

Troon, South Ayrshire. Large bronze Britannia (Gilbert) stands on the seafront facing the sea, where local people died in the First World War.

Uig, Western Isles. Naval and military pylon erected on Lewis in 1999.

Whalsay, Shetland. Unusual crenellated plinth and cross.

WALES

Abergavenny, Monmouthshire. 'Tommy', arms akimbo, rests on his rifle (Ledward).

Aberystwyth, Ceredigion. Humanity on a tall column on the seafront.

Betws-y-Coed, Conwy. Oakley Quarry workers' slate monolith (O. Roberts).

Brecon, Powys. Cathedral, South Wales Borderers regimental memorials.

Builth Wells, Powys. Town cross with military figures on guard around the base.

Caernarfon, Gwynedd. 'Caernarfon Heroes', Town Square.

Cardiff. Welsh National War Memorial, Alexandra Park. Charge of the Light Brigade

(Goscombe John) – Tredegar Memorial, Cathays Park. Boer War winged Victory (Toft), Law Courts. St John's Church: Burma Star Window. Llandaff Cathedral: 'Sons of Llandaff' monument (Goscombe John).

Carmarthen. General Nott (E. Davis) cast from the bronze of cannon captured at Maharajpur in 1843. Crimea monument (Richardson), Lammas Street. Boer War memorial, Guildhall. Priory Street Hospital, bandaged 'Tommy' (Goscombe John). Picton Terrace, 60 foot obelisk to General Picton, killed at Waterloo, 1815.

Chirk, Wrexham. Idiosyncratic obelisk (Gill).

Cilmeri, Powys. 15 foot granite monolith to Llewelyn, the last Welsh Prince, killed here in 1282.

Dinorwic, Gwynedd. Clocktower.

Lampeter, Carmarthenshire. Soldier hero (Goscombe John).

Llandrindod Wells, Powys. Mourning 'Tommy' (B. Lloyd).

Llanfairpwll, Anglesey. Former Conway Naval School chapel, rolls of honour including Lieutenant I. E. (Titch) Fraser, VC, a submarine commander, and Lieutenant Commander Skinner, killed while commanding HMS *Amethyst* on the Yangtse.

Llangefni, Anglesey. Village clock.

Merthyr Vale, Merthyr Tydfil. 'Tommy' triumphant (G. Thomas).

Monmouth. Kymin: naval 'temple' to Nelson and other admirals, successful against the French in the 1790s.

Newport. Cenotaph; Newport Battalion memorial tablet, Civic Centre.

Swansea. Cenotaph. D-Day memorial, Christ Church.

Tenby, Pembrokeshire. Cenotaph and memorial gates.

Tredegar, Blaenau Gwent. 'Tommy' presents arms below a cross (Newbury Trent).

Tywyn, Gwynedd. War Memorial Hospital.

Valley, Anglesey. RAF memorial window in parish church.

Wrexham. Royal Welsh Fusiliers Monument, 'Tommy' shielded by his eighteenth-century counterpart (Goscombe John). Llay Church memorial, Hightown Barracks.

64

Index

Angell, John 11
Anton, Gunther 34
Artists' Rifles 15, 38
Arts and Crafts Movement 30
Ashford (Kent) 14
Baker, Herbert 44
Battle of Britain 2, 32, 33
Battlefield burials 10, 25, 31, 41
Beaconsfield 26
Bell, John 8
Benson, Peter 48
Birmingham 1, 43
Birnie Rhind, William 9
Blackpool 22
Blitz 17, 33
Blomfield, Sir Reginald 26, 44, 45
Boer War 9, 12, 20, 24, 37, 43
Brown, Cecil 39
Brown, Kellock 48
Budden, Lionel 27
Bude 13
Burma Star Association 17, 34
Burnet, Sir John 13
Bushey 10
Cambridge 16
Canterbury Cathedral 28, 40
Cardiff 34, 38
Carlisle Cathedral 30
Carrick, Alexander 48
Cassidy, John 22, 48
Cavell, Edith 44
Cenotaphs 13, 27, 38, 45
Challcott, George 9
Charles I 4
Charles II 4, 5
Chatham 32, 40, 41, 42
Chattri 39
Coade stone 6, 42
Comper, Sir Ninian 38
Coventry 22, 35
Crecy 29
Crimea 8, 23, 41
Croix de Guerre 39
Cross of Sacrifice 26, 32
Cyclists 40, 49
D-Day Museum 41
Dambusters 18
De Comyn, Andy 58
Derby 33
Dunkirk 31
Durham Cathedral 24, 37
Easton, Hugh 32, 33, 45
Edinburgh 3, 6, 9
Eleanor crosses 25
Elveden 23
Epstein, Jacob 2, 46
Exeter 11
Falklands 18, 19
Far East POWs 17, 19, 40
Faversham 13
Firefighters 17
Flodden 29

Frampton, Sir George 43, 44
Free French 62
Freemasons Hall 17
George, Saint 10, 11, 23, 31
Gibbons, Grinling 5
Gill, Eric 25, 46
Glasgow 13
Gloucester Cathedral 29
Gordon, General Charles 41
Goscombe John, Sir William 10, 42, 43
Graves, Robert 47
Great Western Railway 44
Great Yarmouth 6
Guards Memorial 8
Herne Bay 37
Hill, Vernon 18
Home Guard 31
Horses 14
Huntingdon 49
Imperial Camel Corps 39
Imperial (Commonwealth) War Graves Commission 11, 16, 25, 26, 27, 35, 39, 44, 45, 46, 50
Imperial Yeomanry 9
Jagger, Charles 15, 43, 44
Jones, Adrian 42, 43
Jutland 11
Kabul 8
Kennington, Eric 38, 46, 47
Keswick 12
Ketton 24
Kitchener, Field Marshal Herbert 11, 40
Korea 17, 21
Lanterne des Morts 22, 26
Lawrence of Arabia 38
Ledward, Gilbert 22, 46, 47
Leighton Buzzard 21
Lichgates 26, 40
Liverpool 27, 43
London & South Western Railway 11
Lorimer, Sir Robert 44, 46
Loughborough Carillon 36
Lutyens, Sir Edwin 13, 16, 26, 27, 44, 45
Maidstone 7
Margate 9
Marsden, Walter 13
Maufe, Sir Edward 16, 18, 32, 45, 46
Mills, John W. 17
'Missing' 11, 15, 18, 45, 50
Moreton 34, 38
Napoleonic POWs 7
National Memorial Arboretum 19, 40, 48, 58
National Servicemen 17
Nelson, Admiral Horatio 1, 4, 6, 42
New Forest 24
'New Sculpture' 42
Newcastle 10

'Old Contemptibles' 10, 14
Oldham 16
Oundle School 45
Oxford 27
Pearson, Lionel 15, 47, 48
Pegram, A. Bertram 38
Plymouth 21
Poole, Henry 45, 46
Port of London Authority 33
Portsmouth 19, 41, 45
Pre-Raphaelites 30, 31
Prestwich & Sons 22
Reid Dick, Sir William 10, 44
Rochester Cathedral 30
Rodin, Auguste 42, 49
Royal Hospital, Chelsea 5, 50
Royal Marines 19, 43
Royal School of Military Engineering 41
Runnymede Monument 18, 35
St John's Ambulance 25, 37
Scott, Sir Giles Gilbert 23
Scott, Kathleen 49
Scottish National Memorial 2, 46
Sheffield 37
Shot at dawn 58
Shrewsbury 38
Simonds, George 8
Snell & Co 48
Somme 10
Southampton 13, 45
Spencer, Stanley 47
Spitfires 33
Stewart & Co 48
Stockport Art Gallery 47
Stourbridge 22
Sueno's Stone 20
Szlumper, A. W. 11
Tanks 14, 15, 22
Thornton Cleveleys 12
Toft, Albert 16, 42, 43
Trench art 37
Victoria Crosses 46
Voluntary Aid Detachments 25
'Waterloo' churches 5, 7
Waterloo station 11
Wellington, Field Marshal Arthur, Duke of 42
Welsh National Monument 38
Westmacott, Sir Richard 1, 42
Westmacott, Richard (Jnr) 7
Wheeler, Sir Charles 45
Whiffen, Charles 10, 16
Whistler, Laurence 34, 35
White & Sons 48
Wilkins, William 6
Willement, Thomas 29
Women 10, 11, 15, 17, 25, 32, 33, 39, 44, 46, 49
Wood, F. Derwent 12, 44
Wren, Sir Christopher 5
Zulus 30